Wise and Witty

Wise and Witty
Observations of a Word Watcher

Joan Harkness

André Deutsch

First published in Great Britain 1998
by André Deutsch Limited
76 Dean Street
London W1V 5HA
www.vci.co.uk

André Deutsch is a company of VCI plc

A Catalogue record for this book is available
from the British Library

Book design by Harold King

ISBN 0 233 99353 3

Typeset by Derek Doyle & Associates
Mold, Flintshire.
Printed by Butler and Tanner,
Frome and London.

To the two people who meant so much to me:
My mother and Rob.

THE LAWLESS LANGUAGE

The English language, as we all know, has many idiosyncrasies. Perhaps they are best expressed in this verse, variously called 'Plurals', 'The King's English' and 'The Law Less English language'.

> We'll begin with a box and the plural is boxes;
> But the plural of ox should be oxen not oxes.
> Then one fowl is a goose, but two are called geese.
> Yet the plural of mouse should never be meese!
> You may find a lone mouse or a whole nest of mice,
> But the plural of house is houses, not hise!
> If the plural of man is always called men,
> Why shouldn't the plural of pan be called pen?
> If I speak of a foot, and you show me your feet,
> And I give you a boot – would a pair be called beet?
> If one is a tooth, and a whole set are teeth,
> Why should not the plural of booth be called beeth?
> Then one may be that and three would be those,
> Yet hat in the plural would never be hose;
> And the plural of cat is cats, and not cose!
> We speak of a brother, and also of brethren,
> But although we say mother we never say methren!

Then the masculine pronouns are he, his and him,
But imagine the feminine, she, shis and shim!
So English, I fancy you all will agree,
Is the funniest language you ever did see.

Having just given birth to my first baby, I had been returned to my hospital room where my room mate was finishing her supper, after being delivered of her tenth child a few hours earlier. I couldn't wait to talk about my experiences. 'What did you have?' I asked.

'Mince,' she replied.

HEARTS OF OAK

During repairs to Westminster Hall in London after the war, the 500-year-old beams in the roof were found to be rotten. To strike a nice historical echo, the oaks to provide the replacement beams were cut from the estates of the Earl of Warwick, whose distant ancestor had provided the original beams in 1394. When a magnificent oak – huge, straight and unimaginably old – was being selected, the earl's forester consulted his survey. 'Ah, no, not that one,' he said. 'You see, we refused that one the first time.'

Bernard Levin in the *Daily Mail*

TELEVISION IS THE
CULTURE OF LOWBROWS

'The one thing that all concerned with mass media must recognize is that the common man has the right to be common,' Mr Lee Loevinger, a member of the Federal Communications Commission told the New Jersey's Broadcaster's Association in an address in Atlantic City.

'There is more nonsense, garbage and hogwash spoken, written and printed about television than about any other single subject, with the possible exception of sex,' he said.

'The more I see of television the more I dislike and defend it. Television is not for me, but for many others who do like it, but who have no time for many things I like.

'Television is a golden goose that lays scrambled eggs, and it is futile and probably fatal to beat it for not laying caviar. Anyway, more people like scrambled eggs than caviar.

'Television should be recognized for what it is,' he continued, 'the literature of the illiterate, the culture of the lowbrows, the wealth of the poor, the privilege of the under-privileged and the exclusive club of the excluded masses.'

If it were forced to admit the élite it would lose its exclusivity for the masses. 'This, as the clubby elite should know, will destroy its value for those who belong to it,' he said.

It would not, and should not, take the place of the school, the church, the home or even the parents, but it was sometimes a useful baby-sitter.

Mr Loevinger saw little chance of improvement in future. Television would only change with public taste, for better or worse.

Times Correspondent

PROOF

'Photographs – Do Not Bend', wrote the sender carefully. But somewhere in the post he was proved wrong. On the crumpled envelope someone had scrawled: 'They do, you know!'

'Sir, I am glad to say that my husband, reported missing, is now dead.'

This letter is one of many from the British public which are being shown to London civil servants taking a course in good writing.

Here are other samples from the files of the Pension Office:

'I want some money as quick as you can send it. I have been in bed with my doctor all week and he does not seem to be doing me any good.'

'Mrs R has no clothes and has not had any for a year. The clergy have been visiting her.'

'Re your enquiry, the teeth in the top are all right, but the ones in the bottom are hurting horribly.'

'Unless I get my husband's money, I shall be forced to lead an immortal life.'

Iana Reuter

In a Tanzanian village, an anti US parade was said to have been led by a brass band which, having been trained by American missionaries, could play only one tune: 'The Stars and Stripes Forever.'

Time

Film star Jean Harlow, then at the top of her career, had been introduced to that tartar Lady Asquith and kept calling her Margot. In inimitable fashion, Lady Asquith eventually remarked: 'My dear, the "T" is silent, as in "Harlow".'

'HI HI, YOU FOOL'

Literal translation of extracts from the Japanese Highway Code of some years ago make fascinating reading. But should you be visiting Japan, I suggest you check to see if these rules are still operative before you go yelling 'Hi hi', or tootling with vigour.

'At the rise of the hand of the policeman, stop rapidly. Do not pass him or otherwise disrespect him.

When a passenger of the foot hoves in sight, tootle the horn. Trumpet to him melodiously at first. If he is still an obstacle to your passage, tootle him with vigour, expressing by word or the mouth the warning 'Hi hi'.

Beware of the wandering horse that he shall not take fright as you pass him. Do not explode the exhaust box at him. Go soothingly by, or stop at the roadside until he passes away.

Give big space to the festive dog. Avoid entanglement of the dog with your wheel spokes.'

Carpenter, the *Rhodesia Herald*

My husband, who is the loan manager of one of our local banks, tells of a young woman who applied for a loan with which she wished to secure a divorce. He told her that he did not make loans for divorces, only for appliances of all kinds, cars and home improvements.

'But, sir,' she said earnestly, 'this would be a home improvement.'

CHILDREN LEARN WHAT THEY LIVE

If a child lives with criticism, He learns to condemn.
If a child lives with hostility, He learns to fight.
If a child lives with ridicule, He learns to be shy.
If a child lives with shame, He learns to feel guilty.
If a child lives with tolerance, He learns to be patient
If a child lives with encouragement, He learns confidence.
If a child lives with praise, He learns to appreciate.
If a child lives with fairness, He learns justice.
If a child lives with security, He learns to have faith.
If a child lives with approval, He learns to like himself.
If a child lives with acceptance and friendship,
He learns to find love in the world.

Dorothy Law Nolte

In Rheims, an innkeeper opened a bottle of Champagne from his wine cellar and found this note in the packing: 'Will the person who drinks this champagne and finds my photo here please write to me. I am seventeen and looking for a husband.'

The inkeeper wrote and received this reply: 'Alas! Your champagne was bottled in 1956. Wine can wait and age ten years in confidence, but a woman cannot.'

N W

EXCUSE ME

Vice-Admiral Hyman Rickover, then the US Navy's nuclear propulsion expert, who was known as a no-time-wasting man of action, had this poster on the door of his office.

The List Below Is the Current Popularity Rating for Excuses. To Save Time For Me and Yourself, Please Give Your Excuse by Number.

1 I thought I told you.
2 That's the way we've always done it.
3 No one told me to go ahead.
4 I didn't think it was very important.
5 I'm so busy I just can't get around to it.
6 Why bother? The admiral won't swallow it.
7 I didn't know you were in a hurry for it.
8 That's his job, not mine.
9 I'm waiting for an OK.
10 I forgot.
11 That's not in my department.
12 How did I know this was different?
13 Wait till the boss comes back and ask him.

H G Rickover (circa 1966)

A US Navy wife, whose officer husband was on duty in London, reported: We have a sign marked NAVY on the window of our car. While shopping in Mayfair one day, I parked in a side street. When I returned I found a note under my windscreen wiper: 'Kindly tie up ahead or astern of the No Parking sign on your port beam.'

Page Griffin

An advertisement in a Colorado newspaper read: 'Wanted – man to work on nuclear fissionable isotope molecular reactive counters and three-phase cyclotronic uranium synthesizers. No experience necessary.'

Carpenter, *The Rhodesia Herald*

Lewis L Strauss, Chairman of the US Atomic Energy Commission, liked to illustrate, with this story, that invention has not come to the end of its tether.

In the 1870s, a bishop who had charge of a small denominational college made his annual visit and stayed with the principal. The bishop boasted a firm belief that everything that could be invented had been invented. The college head thought otherwise.

'In 50 years,' he said, 'men will learn how to fly like birds.'

The bishop, shocked, replied, 'Flight is reserved for angels and you have been guilty of blasphemy.'

The name of the bishop was Milton Wright and at home he had two small sons – Orville and Wilbur.

New York Times

Last Easter, when I was co-pilot of an airline flight, I put a few coloured hard-boiled eggs in my pocket before leaving, intending to hand them out to the crew. Later, while cruising along at 14,000 feet, I remembered the eggs. My coat was in the overhead rack in the passenger cabin with my cap on top of it. I stepped into the cabin, put my cap on my head, got my coat down from the rack and was starting to unfold it when a woman in an aisle seat, who had been watching me with a somewhat startled expression, asked, 'And where do you think you're going?'

Edmund Crump

A fellow was driving to a mountain resort when a policeman stopped him and said, 'Did you know your rear lights aren't working?' The driver got out of the car, visibly disturbed by this piece of information. The policeman sought to reassure him. 'It's not too much of an offence,' he said. 'Nothing to get upset about.'

'It may not mean much to you,' the driver replied. 'But to me it means I have lost a caravan, a wife and four kids.'

Driving home for the summer holidays, I had packed my tiny foreign car to window level with clothes, books and records. Then I fitted myself into a narrow slit behind the wheel. When I stopped for petrol, a tall attendant bent double to peer in the window. Then straightening up, he beamed approval. 'Nice little four-door suitcase you've got there,' he said.

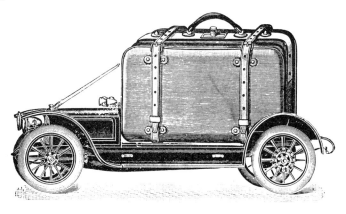

Britain replied to a Soviet demand in the United Nations that it grant immediate independence to the 'original inhabitants' of the islands of Mauritius and the Seychelles in the Indian Ocean, and St Helena in the South Atlantic. To the Russian delegate's denunciations of the British as 'brutal colonizers who shattered the idyllic existence of the indigenous people' of the islands, the United Kingdom made these rejoinders:

'I am afraid the original inhabitants of Mauritius were of the dodo species which is extinct and unable to press its claim to be granted independence on the basis of one bird, one vote. The original inhabitants of the Seychelles were, I believe, giant tortoises, not completely extinct, but they have shown no interest in political advance. The first explorers on St Helena record the presence of pheasants, partridges and terns, but alas, no indigenous inhabitants.'

New York *Herald Tribune* (circa 1964)

A Los Angeles Supreme Court jury awarded Mrs Amy Pawson $42,000 because a pharmacy accidentally gave her sleeping tablets instead of birth control pills. She claimed that as a result she had her fourth child at a time when she could not afford it. Seems that the sleeping pills didn't work too well either.

On a shopping spree, my mother and I saw a fashion exhibition in one of the large stores. Among the more costly items was a gold lamé shirt priced at £250. We told my grandmother about this later, and she, being hard of hearing, burst out: '£250 for an old army shirt? Disgusting!'

At the start of a concert, pianist Artur Schnabel observed that a woman in the front row had dozed off. She slept through the entire performance. When the concert was over, the pianist received an ovation. As he was taking his bows, the woman suddenly awoke. Schnabel leaned forward and said apologetically, 'It was the applause madam. I played as softly as possible.'

And this from the Zimbabwe *Star*:

'Both Chikerema and Nkala are political clowns who would do better if they could find work in the circus business, such as the famous Piccadilly Circus.'

⌐

One day, several winters ago, I arrived at the small factory where I worked to find the furnace had broken down. We were sent home and told that those who wanted to return after the furnace was repaired would be contacted by phone and the company car would pick them up. As I wasn't on the phone, I left the number of the family that lived above me. Two hours later, my upstairs neighbour came looking for me, pale and shaky. She handed me a note which read, 'The heat is on. We are sending someone to get you.'

R T

Middle Age: when the warning to slow down comes from a doctor instead of a policeman.

⌒

The Psychology department at one university recently equipped a common-room where graduate students could relax and meditate. The room was equipped with a coffee maker and all the accompaniments, even individual name-painted cups.

The psychology students were appreciative. A sign soon decorated the common-room notice board: 'Happiness is a Good Cup of Coffee'.

Then another appeared beneath it: 'Security is Having Your Own Cup'.

And, finally: 'Anxiety is Wondering Who Has Been Using It'.

C N

A young man who took a driving test for a motor-scooter licence was told by the examiner to ride three times round a city square. 'Keep alert,' said the examiner, 'because I am going to step off the pavement in front of you to test your braking reactions.'

After three circuits, there was still no sign of the examiner. Failing to find him, the young man finally returned to the test centre to report what had happened.

'It's very unfortunate,' explained the man in charge, 'but I am afraid that your examiner is now on his way to hospital. You see, he stepped out in front of the wrong scooter.'

Warden of New College, Oxford, from 1903 to 1924, the Reverend William Spooner has been immortalized for his amusing lapses of speech, now known as Spoonerisms. His all-time classic was uttered when he summoned an erring undergraduate to his study and said sternly: 'Sir, you have deliberately tasted two whole worms, you have hissed all my mystery lectures and you have been caught fighting a liar in the quad. You will leave by the next town drain.'

Sir Winston Churchill was once asked what he considered desirable qualifications for a budding politician. He assumed his bulldog expression. 'It is the ability,' he rumbled thoughtfully, 'to foretell what is going to happen tomorrow, next month and next year.' He paused, then added, 'And the ability to explain afterwards why it didn't.'

The Wit of Sir Winston, edited by Adam Sykes
(Frewin, London)

In Russia there are no words for 'a' or 'the' and Russians speaking English tend to leave them out. Some time ago, the late Russian poet David Marshak told about his first visit to England. He said that when he stepped off the train at Victoria Station in London, he said to a passer-by, 'Excuse, please, can you tell me what is time?'

'Ah,' said the stranger gravely. 'My friend, you have posed a deep and imponderable question.'

Eddy Gilmore, *The Listener*

An Indian chief of great repute decided to marry, and in the custom of his tribe installed three squaws in separate wigwams a little distance from his own lodging.

During the night he visited them in turn and noticed that while the first two covered their tent floor with buffalo hides the third one utilized a hippopotamus hide.

In due course the first two squaws each presented him with a fine son, but the third had twin boys – which proves Pythagoras's theorem, 'The squaw on the hippopotamus is equal to the sum of the squaws on the other two hides.'

A story told at a skydiving club is about the member who participated in a night-time jump, wearing red and white flashing lights to prevent mid-air collision with other members. He mistook a well-lit area for his predetermined target and steered his parachute towards it. Upon landing, he realized his mistake and walked over to a woman who had watched his descent. With his lights still flashing, he asked where he was. The woman, obviously shaken by the event, quickly replied, 'Earth!'

Learning to pilot a sea plane when he was First Lord of the Admiralty, Winston Churchill was bringing his craft in to land when it suddenly lost speed and belly-flopped into the sea.

'You should maintain your speed all the way down to the surface,' his instructor commented respectfully.

'I thought you had taken over,' replied the distinguished pupil.

Seeing their misunderstanding, his instructor said, 'It seems we were falling between two stools.'

Replied Winston, 'More like stalling between two fools.'

G Cardwell

How about this for mystic maths:

A sultan had 17 elephants. In his will he left

1/2 to his eldest son
1/3 to his second
1/9 to his last

When he read this the lawyer was stumped. So he borrowed an elephant from a neighbour to make the number up to 18 and gave:

1/2 to the first son
1/3 to the next
1/9 to the youngest

That added up to 17, so he returned the neighbour's elephant.

Nubar Gulbenkian was one of the world's wealthiest men, and he enjoyed good living. He once bought a fabulous car in London and, in describing it, said, 'It has disc brakes, whatever that is. It has automatic transmission, whatever that is. It has power steering, whatever that is. And it can turn on a sixpence – whatever *that* is.'

Leonard Lyons

It will probably come as a surprise to present-day motorists to know that the ancient Romans had to pass a strict test before they were issued with a licence to drive their chariots or wagons. At one stage all women's licences were withdrawn because of the number of cases of dangerous driving that came before the magistrates. This ban on women drivers lasted nearly 20 years, during which time the ladies waged furious campaigns to have it repealed. In the end Cicero was persuaded to plead their case in the Senate and licences were finally restored to women. To celebrate their victory the ladies held a monster chariot rally outside Rome. Before it ended, five competitors had been killed and scores of spectators seriously injured.

Parking was also a problem in ancient Rome. The situation became so bad at the time of Julius Caesar that he prohibited all parking in the centre of Rome during the day. This move led to the establishment of chariot parks run on similar lines to our modern car parks.

To keep traffic moving Caesar also introduced one-way streets and built raised pavements above the level of the road to protect pedestrians. In the open country all traffic drove on the left, so that drivers could more easily wield whips in their right hands. To prevent speeding in the towns, traffic was made to drive on the right. All the roads were well signposted and in the country showed not only the distance between towns but also the distance to Rome; hence the saying 'All roads lead to Rome'.

It is unlikely that anyone goes through a day's conversation without quoting Shakespeare. Once in a while we realize we are doing this but, most of the time, we lift his lines to season our speech and sharpen our opinions without the slightest thought of the source.

When you call a man a 'rotten apple', a 'blinking idiot' or a 'popinjay' . . . when you say he 'bears a charmed life' or is 'hoist with his own petard' . . . when you proclaim him 'a man of few words' . . .

When you speak of 'cold comfort', 'grim necessity', 'bag and baggage', 'the mind's eye', 'holding your tongue', 'suiting the action to the words' . . . when you refer to your 'salad days' or 'heart of hearts' when you lament 'the beginning of the end', 'life's uncertain voyage' or 'the unkindest cut of all', you are quoting Shakespeare!

When you use such expressions as 'poor but honest' 'one fell swoop', 'as luck would have it', 'the short and the long of it', 'neither here nor there', 'what's done is done' . . . When you say something 'smells to Heaven' or is 'Greek to me' or it's a 'mad world' or 'not in my book' . . . When you complain that you 'haven't slept a wink' or that your family is 'eating you out of house and home' or you've 'seen better days' . . . When you speak of a coward 'showing his heels' or having 'no stomach for a fight' . . . When you nod wisely and say 'Love is blind' or

'Truth will come to light' or 'The World is my oyster' you are borrowing your *bon mot* from the Bard.

Shakespeare was the greatest cliché inventor of all time. Without him to put the words in our mouths the English language would have a lean and hungry look.

Reader's Digest (circa 1964)

After the instructor's lecture on parachute jumping, one recruit asked nervously, 'What happens if the 'chute fails to open?'

'That,' replied the instructor, 'is what is known as jumping to conclusions.'

In England, a bus full of Americans pulled to a stop at Runnymede. One passenger demanded of the guide, 'What happened here?'

'This is where the Magna Carta was signed.'

'When?' asked the American.

'1215', replied the guide.

Looking at his watch, the tourist said to his wife, 'My goodness, Edna, we missed it by 20 minutes!'

A long-range Maritime Command aircraft was conducting an uneventful surveillance flight off Canada's east coast. Suddenly, the tedium was broken as the navigator issued terse instructions to the pilot for radical course alterations 60° to starboard, then 120° to port, then 60° to starboard again in rapid succession.

Puzzled and curious as to the need for the unscheduled course changes, the pilot asked the reason.

'I just spilled coffee over my plotting chart,' replied the navigator, 'and I'll be damned if we're going to fly through that mess.'

'After the party this chap took me home and gave me a beautiful mink coat.'
    'What did you have to do?'
    'Just alter the sleeves.'

Girl pouring drinks at party: 'Say when.'
    Young man: 'As soon as the party's over.'

The following appeared after Picasso's death.

DISTORTION

' "I have always maintained that every artist is a propagandist," wrote George Orwell, "he is trying directly or indirectly to impose a vision of life."

The vision imposed on the world of art by Pablo Picasso, was one of distortion that elevated the irrational and the obscene to lofty heights. No man in modern times did more to undermine aesthetic beauty and flowing form than Picasso. If he was great, it was a greatness for propagandizing the cult of the ugly, the deformed and the destructive.

Picasso was a special breed among artistic hypocrites . . . He once observed: "Art is a saleable commodity . . . I'm only a clown, a mountebank. I have understood my time and I have exploited the imbecility, the vanity and the greed of my contemporaries."

One must laugh with Picasso at the way he managed to con the entire world into accepting and paying handsome sums for doodlings, scribblings and grotesque renderings on canvas elevated to the status of art . . .

He and others destroyed painting and nobility, substituting instead deformity and depersonalization. When one wonders why the world around us seems so decadent and destructive, one principal source of this moral and aesthetic decay is the mental illness called modern art.

Those bowing down to Picasso and praising him as great at his death are bowing down to intellectual barbarism, and are paying homage to institutionalized insanity.'

Jeffrey St John, *Spectrum*

One day, one of my journalistic colleagues asked the rest of us if we'd heard of a mythical American called Phil D Basket, who exhorted New Yorkers to throw their litter into bins rather than the street.

From Phil D Basket it was but a short step to Mahatma Kote, the Indian cloakroom attendant, Fay Slifter, the plastic surgeon; while pretty soon we realized that if Warren Peace was the biographer of Tolstoy, then Bertha D Blews must be a jazz singer, just as Rudy Day was a regretful husband and Lottie Cairs his neglected wife.

Very soon nobody got any work done at all. Men would sit up far into the night reading dictionaries for inspiration and come in next day, red-eyed but triumphant, shouting: 'What about Bosun Arrows, the nautical archer, Walter Wall, the carpet salesman, Stan Dandyliver, the highwayman . . .'

Then our lives became crowded with some very strange people, many of them foreign, like Hans Neezen-Boomzerdayzee, the Dutch folksinger, a dance-hall cleaner named Artur di Ballwass-Ova, Ann Tzinner-Pantz, the Middle European contortionist, Beau Neidel, the lazy German fop and – inevitably – the Norwegian bartender, Lars Torders.

Letter to the *Guardian*

Party guest: 'How did you get that scar on the bridge of your nose?'
   'From glasses.'
   'Why don't you use contact lenses?'
   'They don't hold enough beer.'

By the time a man has money to burn, the fire has gone out.

A 200-pound man crawled up on his roof to retrieve his son's toy soldier-and-parachute. After gingerly inching across the steep roof, he lost his grip and slid off. As the ambulance attendants were placing him on a stretcher, he came to. With a feeble grin he muttered, 'I bet you're sorry I'm such a heavyweight.'

One attendant, looking at him still clutching his son's toy, responded, 'I bet you're sorry you jumped with that tiny little parachute.'

Reader's Digest (circa 1965)

⌒

A Greek restaurateur in Montreal had his own book-keeping system. He kept his accounts payable in a cigar-box on the left-hand side of his cash register, his daily cash returns in the cash register, and his receipts for paid bills in another cigar-box on the right. When his youngest son graduated as a chartered accountant, he was appalled by his father's primitive methods. 'I don't know how you can run a business that way,' he said. 'How do you know what your profits are?'

'Well, son,' the father replied, 'when I got off the boat from Greece, I had nothing but the trousers I was wearing. Today, your brother is a doctor, you are an accountant and your sister is a speech therapist. Your mother and I have a nice car, a city house, a country home. We have a good business, and everything is paid for. So, you add all that together, subtract the trousers, and there's your profit.'

A bedtime story told to a nine year old went like this: 'When the little frog rescued her golden ball from the well, the princess was so grateful that she let him spend the night in her room. The next morning when she woke up the frog had turned into a handsome prince and they were married and lived happily ever after.'

The child looked dubious.

'Don't you believe the story?' I asked.

'No,' she replied, 'I don't. And I'll bet her mother didn't either.'

A plumber who wanted to use hydrochloric acid to unblock clogged pipes wrote to the authorities asking what they thought about it. A departmental head replied: 'The efficacy of hydrochloric acid is indisputable. However its corrosive action is incompatible with metallic permanence.'

This confused the simple plumber, who wrote back: 'Thanks for the advice; I'll order some right away.'

Somewhat disturbed the departmental head replied: 'Regret your lack of comprehension, but I must inform you that the resulting toxic residue makes affirmative reply still invalid.'

Now thoroughly stumped, the plumber wrote: 'Sorry about the invalid but thanks for your help. I'll start using the acid next week.'

So the frantic departmental head did what he should have done in the first place. He sent a wire saying: 'Don't use the stuff. It'll eat the hell out of the pipes.'

Rhodesia Herald

On an African safari, the guide was asked how to keep from being attacked by wild animals at night. 'Just carry a lighted torch,' he suggested.

'Does it really work?' the questioner persisted.

'That depends,' explained the guide, 'On how fast you carry it.'

During a geography lecture, the professor was explaining that the term 'backward' is no longer used when describing the economy of a primitive state. In order to avoid hurting the pride of such countries, the term 'under-developed' is considered preferable. Looking round the lecture hall, he saw one student who didn't seem to understand the psychological implications of the two terms:

'Well, Miss Turner,' he asked, 'which would you rather be – under-developed or backward?'

'Backward, sir!' was her quick reply to the red-faced professor.

LAMENT

Alas, alack. Oh deary me
I am so fat, as you can see.
For girth has spread with middle age,
And mirror image doth enrage.
Methought an ode I would compose
About sad growth of adipose.
I eat no butter, nor yet marge
But somehow still stay very large.
I can't remember fish and chips
Yet lack of it don't change my hips.
When offered cake I deign to risk it
But have been known to scorn a biscuit.
I ration bread to minute crust
Though still retain a Mae West bust.
I forgo puds, say no to cream
While broader grows both thigh and beam.
Consumed no sugar since the war
Yet rounded tum you can't ignore.
Milkless my tea, and coffee neat,
Dislike all wine both dry and sweet.
What do I live on? you might ask . . .
A calorie count's my nightly task.
Eight hundred is my usual score,
Just can't reduce it any more.

Of lettuce leaves I've had my share,
Am sick to death of rabbit's fare.
I daily walk for exercise
But grub, it won't metabolize.
I pen this poem with contrition . . .
You see, at work, I teach Nutrition.

Woman magazine

An army unit received a barrel of beer in Iraq during the First World War. The officers tried the brew, then passed it to the NCOs. They tried it and gave it to the troops. An officer came by as it was being drunk and asked, 'How's the beer, men?'

'Just right, thank you sir,' replied a private. 'If it had been any better we wouldn't have got it, and if it had been any worse we couldn't have drunk it.'

A report by the Southern California Medical Association pointed out that proper weight control and physical fitness cannot be attained by dieting alone. A particular problem is faced by the person who spends most of his or her day in a sedentary occupation. Too many of these people fail to realize that calories can be burned off in their hundreds by engaging in strenuous exercises that are common to office workers. The following is a list of calorie-burning activities, together with the number of calories per hour they consume.

Beating around the bush	75
Jogging your memory	125
Jumping to conclusions	100
Climbing the walls	150
Swallowing your pride	50
Passing the buck	25
Grasping at straws	75
Blowing your own trumpet	100
Throwing your weight around	
(Depending upon your weight)	50–300
Dragging your heels	100
Pushing your luck	250
Making mountains out of molehills	500
Flying off the handle	225
Hitting the nail on the head	50
Turning the other cheek	75

Wading through paperwork	300
Bending over backwards	75
Jumping on the bandwagon	200
Balancing the books	23
Beating your head against a wall	150
Running around in circles	350
Fishing for compliments	50
Climbing the ladder of success	750
Pulling out the stoppers	75
Adding fuel to the fire	150
Pouring salt on the wound	50
Wrapping it up at day's end	12

The long-haired member of the family, who suddenly had his hair cut, was asked, 'How much weight did you lose in that operation?'

'About 60 kilograms,' he said. 'I got my mother off my back.'

A faith-healer met a pal of his who said his brother was very sick. 'He's not sick, he just thinks he's sick. Remember that,' said the faith-healer.

A month later they met again, and the faith-healer asked about the man's brother.

'He's much worse now,' he said. 'He thinks he's dead.'

Nowadays, work has lost many traditional characteristics and so has play. Play has increasingly been transformed into organized sport and sport, in turn, increasingly resembles work, in the arduous practice and preparation it entails, and in the actual economic productivity. In a final paradox, only those sports which began as work – that is, hunting and fishing – are now dominated by the spirit of play.

Sport and Society

He drove his German-made car, of Swedish steel with an interior of Argentinian leather, to a petrol station where he filled it up with Arab petrol shipped in a Liberian tanker, and bought two French tyres composed of rubber from Sri Lanka.

At home, he dropped his Moroccan briefcase, hung up his Scottish tweed coat, took off his Italian shoes and Irish wool socks, along with his shirt made of American cotton, and donned his robe from Hong Kong with matching slippers from Taiwan.

More comfortable now, he poured a hot cup of Brazilian coffee into an English mug, set it down on a Swazi place mat, which was on an Irish linen tablecloth atop a Spanish table, varnished with linseed oil from India.

Then, he filled his Austrian pipe with Turkish tobacco, lit it with a lighter manufactured in France, picked up his American fountain pen and wrote a letter to his member of parliament, demanding to know why the price of goods in Britain was rising so rapidly.

'Do you have any four-volt, two-watt bulbs?'
    'For what?'
    'No, two.'
    'Two what?'
    'Yes.'
    'No.'

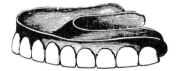

On a dental-assistant course, we took dental X-rays of willing subjects. Naturally, we shielded the patients with lead aprons. As one student placed the apron on her patient, he asked what it was for. 'To protect your genes,' she explained.

'Oh, that's all right,' the young man replied. 'They're old anyway.'

A host of strange euphemisms is creeping into the English language. The *Sunday Times* once told of a businessman who disliked the word 'unemployment', preferring the phrase 'men liberated for other tasks'. The *Financial Times* quoted a company report which stated that trading results showed a 'considerable disimprovement'.

Across the Atlantic, matters are even worse. In a letter to *Punch*, Ian Masters reports these gems from the United States:

Pollution: external environmental diseconomy.
Jail: penitentiary premises.
Teacher: instructional communicator.
Typing pool: stenographic battery.

Canadians, he adds, are not even born any more; they 'enter the life cycle'. What's more, when they are sacked they acquire the status of 'special retirement'.

Late one night, a few days after issuing instructions on proper telephone etiquette, a young Navy lieutenant dialled what he thought was the charthouse. He was greeted with a sleepy, 'Yes? What is it?' Testily, the young officer launched into a lecture on the proper military way to answer a phone, then said, 'Now let's start again. Pretend your phone has just rung.'

'Very well,' replied the voice. 'Captain's cabin, Captain speaking, sir.'

⌐

When two women returned to their car after attending a meeting, they discovered a fire smouldering under the back seat. Unable to find a fire extinguisher, or even a phone to call for help with, they simply drove the car to the nearest fire-station. 'You know,' one of the firemen remarked after the small blaze had been extinguished, 'we don't get very much drive-in business.'

Victor Borge, pianist and comedian, announced at the close of a show: 'I wish to thank my mother and father who made this show possible, and my five children who made it necessary.'

～

Determined to see the world, John signed on to a Norwegian freighter as a deckhand. He was being trained as a helmsman and his first lesson was given by the mate, a seasoned but gentle white-haired seafarer.

John was holding the heading he had been given when the mate ordered. 'Come starboard.'

Pleased at knowing immediately which way starboard was, John left the helm and walked over to his instructor. The mate had an incredulous look on his face as the helm swung freely, but he merely asked politely, 'Could you bring the ship with you?'

A film technician spent several months in the Belgian Congo filming *The Roots of Heaven*. While he was there, he collected a trunkful of shrunken heads which he decided might be worth something. So when he returned home, he rang up a large departmental store asking 'To whom do I speak about selling some shrunken heads?'

The switchboard operator told him to wait a moment, then there was a clicking sound and a firm, business-like voice said, 'This is the Head Buyer speaking.'

Chinese brand names can present problems when their goods are exported. These names include: 'White Elephant Auto Parts'; 'Pansy Men's Clothing'; 'Junk Chemicals' and 'Fang Fang Lipstick.'

The chairman of a girls' private school had made a lengthy and boring speech as usual. Then came prize-giving.

'And what are you going to do when you leave school?' he asked one sixth-former who came up for her prize.

'Well, sir, I was thinking of going straight home.'

⌒

School report: 'French: Richard sets himself a remarkably low standard, which he fails consistently to maintain.'

One good thing about small cars: You can squeeze twice as many of them into a traffic jam.

Nothing is harder for some people than to park both ends of a car.

The easiest way to refold a road map is differently.

Who does work?

Who does the work? In view of the current financial crisis, and the ever-increasing cost of living, these figures may be of interest. Their accuracy is immaterial; it's the idea that counts.

Population of the country	6,000,000
People aged 65 and over	700,000
Balance left to do the work	5,300,000
People under the age of 16	3,100,000
Balance left to do the work	2,200,000
People working for the Government	400,000
Balance left to do the work	1,800,000
People in hospitals and asylums	4,356
People in the Senate	23
People in Parliament	66
People in prison or detention	8,789
People in sheltered employment or on the railways	24,679
People working for municipalities	88,888
Unemployed	673,197
Others who won't work anyway	1,000,000
Balance left to do the work	2

You and I must therefore put our shoulders to the wheel and put much more effort into it. Especially you, as I am fed up with running this country on my own.

'THANK YOU, I'M FINE'

There is nothing the matter with me
– I'm as healthy as I can be.
I have arthritis in both my knees
And when I talk, I talk with a wheeze.
My pulse is weak and my blood is thin,
But I'm awfully well for the shape I'm in.
Arch supports I have for my feet
Or I would not be able to walk on the street.
Sleep is denied me night after night
But every morning I find I'm all right!
My memory's failing, my head's in a spin,
But I'm wonderfully well for the shape I'm in.
The moral is this, as my tale I unfold
That for you and me who are growing old,
It's better to say 'I'm fine', with a grin
Than let people know the state you're in.
How do I know that my youth is all spent?
Well, my 'Get up and go' has got up and went.
But I really don't mind when I think with a grin
Of all the grand places my 'Get up' has been in.
Old age is golden, I've heard it said,
But sometimes I wonder as I get into bed
With my ears in a drawer, my teeth in a cup,
My eyes on the table until I get up

'Ere sleep overtakes me, I say to myself,
Is there anything else I could lay on the shelf?
Now I am old and have pains in my back,
I walk to the store and puff my way back.
I get up each morning and dust my wits
And pick up the paper and read the 'OBITS',
If my name is not there I know I'm not dead,
So I have a good breakfast and get back into bed.'

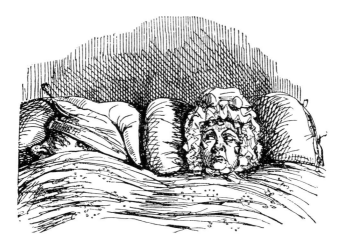

The following were the regulations for a Burnley Cotton Mill office in 1852.

1 Godliness, cleanliness and punctuality are the necessities of a good business.
2 This firm has reduced the hours of work and the clerical staff will now have to be present between the hours of 7am and 6pm on weekdays.
3 Daily prayers will be held each morning in the main office. The clerical staff will be present.
4 Clothing will be of a sober nature. The clerical staff will not disport themselves in raiment of bright colours, nor will they wear hose unless in good repair.
5 Overshoes and topcoats may not be worn in the office, but neck scarves and headwear may be worn in inclement weather.
6 A stove is provided for the clerical staff. Coal and wood must be kept in the locker. It is recommended that each member of the clerical staff bring four pounds of coal each day during the cold weather.
7 No member of the clerical staff may leave the room without permission from Mr Rodgers. The calls of nature are permitted and clerical staff may use the garden below the second gate. This area must be kept in good order.

8 No talking is allowed during business hours.

9 The cravings of tobacco, wines and spirits are a human weakness and, as such, are forbidden to all members of the clerical staff.

10 Now that the hours of business have been drastically reduced, the partaking of food is allowed between 11.30am and noon, but work will not, on any account, cease.

11 Members of the clerical staff will provide their own pens. A new sharpener is available on application to Mr Rodgers.

12 Mr Rodgers will nominate a senior clerk to be responsible for the cleanliness of the main office, and private office, and all boys and juniors will report to him 40 minutes before prayers and will remain after closing hours for similar work. Brushes, brooms, scrubbers and soap are provided by the owners.

13 The new increased wages are hereunder detailed: Junior boys (up to 11 years) 1/4d. Boys (to 14 years) 4/8d. Junior clerks 8/7d. Clerks 10/9d. Senior clerks (after 15 years with the owners) 21/-d.

The owners recognize the generosity of the new Labour Laws but will expect a great rise in output of work to compensate for these near Utopian conditions.

CLOSE TO THE HUMERUS

This one is for the medical profession.

Osseus Tibia met Hernia Phobia at a tennis tourniquet in London. Osseus was fond of moonlight, silver shadows and things like that – a most rheumatic type – and he was so smitten by Hernia's anaemic beauty he thought her the acne of perfection.

He offered to escort her home from the tourniquet, so they caught the tube at a nearby eustachian and went to her flatulence alongside the Alimentary Canal.

There he helped her up the ascending colon to her

rumen, where she played him a medulla oblongata on her clavicle.

Predictably, it wasn't long before Osseus desired to be her lord and mastoid. He asked her to marry him. She agreed, provided that her parents Sir Hydro and Lady Phobia, gave their blessing.

They travelled to the family seat, a noble pile roofed with shingles. Hernia's parents were charming to Osseus, even if a little on the formalin side.

They showed him their pride and joy – the garden – with its fallen arches covered with anthrax; and the herbaceous borders backed by tall bilharzias and anti-toxins.

These were set off by a low-lying rash of glowing smallpox, scarlet fevers and tiny malarias.

On the far side of the verdant gangrene was a wood of witch hazels, while alongside the stream graceful, weeping eczemas grew in profusion.

All was sucrose and glucose until Osseus asked for Hernia's hand. Then Lady Phobia had hysterics and Sir Hydro completely lost his temperature. Both avowed themselves to be highly contraceptive to the scheme.

Sir Hydro, in fact, shouted: 'Gout, you scurvy navel. Abscess yourself, or I shall carve you up with my axilla, you ganglion ape!'

Poor Osseus was shocked to the marrow at this unexpected turn of events, but Hernia stood by him and told him she was prepared to elope with him if that was what he wanted.

'Say ether yes or no,' she pleaded. 'I'll not take the thyroid while you take the low road.'

Osseus, however, had a better idea. 'We shall flee at once to my carbuncle, Sir Cranial Cavity,' he declared forcefully.

At that, Sir Hydro started. 'Is Sir Cranial your soul guardian, then?' he asked. Osseus nodded.

'But then of course you may marry my daughter!' cried Sir Hydro.

Lady Phobia wiped her eyes with her adipose tissue.

After a formal courtship, the happy couple were brought before a clergyman. Osseus said: 'Sinus up.'

The *Daily News,* Durban

Wife, reading astrology book, to husband:

'If you had been born two days later, you would have been kind, generous and witty.'

⌇

A certain lady took great pride in her antique furniture. The slightest stain or scratch on one of her prized relics would stir her otherwise gentle nature to anger. However, she accepted stains and scratches on the normal furniture as a fact of everyday life.

Because of these attitudes, she had a rather unusual way of comforting a woman who had spilled coffee all over one of the ordinary chairs. She turned to the desperately apologetic guest and said, 'Don't worry about that. It's brand new.'

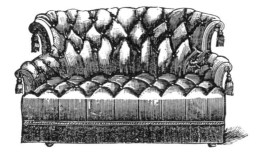

In September 1970, the Skeleton Steel Company of Stratford-upon-Avon, Warwickshire, was closed down by its owners following a one-week strike by their 400 employees. The action was taken by the Chairman, Howard Hicks, after 'careful consideration of my sense of moral and social responsibility as the largest employer of labour in Stratford.'

Mr Hicks then wrote this letter to each employee to explain his decision.

'The one-week strike for higher pay was sufficient to eliminate any profit this company would have made. The new rate of pay, which was the very lowest your representatives would accept, has now priced this company out of the market; it is impossible to compete with other companies in the same business.

I am sure you will appreciate that if a local supermarket got an ultimatum from their staff that they had to have a considerable increase in pay or they would strike, the supermarket would have to raise its prices above others to meet its wages bill. It is common sense that your wives and mothers would immediately shop elsewhere where they could buy their goods cheaper. This is precisely the situation this pay increase has placed Skeleton Steel in.

I hope that whoever advised you that the company could stand pay increases of this sort will now be able to help you to get work at that rate of pay within reasonable travelling distance of your homes.

The company would have attempted to carry on even with the enormous increase in pay if we had been able to make some increased productivity bargain with your negotiators. This was categorically refused. The company cannot do the impossible.

Greater prosperity does not happen, it has to be worked for, and it is only with higher productivity that we will get a higher standard of living. Increased rates of pay without increased productivity only lead to unnecessary inflation. I am desperately sorry that this has had to happen, but the world does not owe Britain a living and the country does not owe Skeleton Steel a living.'

Letter to the *Director* magazine, London (circa 1971)

A sign along a highway in America read: 'Stop at the Reptile Farm! See the Huge Python, the Murderous Rattler in the Pit of Death! A Children's Paradise.'

∽

Some examples of 'Europhrases' displayed at the Stokes Bay Sailing Club

Committee Boat: Die Grosseboot mit lotza Phlagz und Bangenwerks.

Officer of the Day: Der Oberfuhrer der Tag mit der Kap und Shoutentube.

General Recall: Die Vasderhell vasdas earschplitten Bangen.

Mainsail: Das Grossenflapper.

Boom: Der Grossenflapper bonzschplitten Schtick.

Tiller: Die puschenpuller Schtick fur Vich-vay gangen.

Launching Trolley: Das Boot in Wasser gangen Wagen.

Helmsman: Der Dumkopf mit puschenpuller Schtick vas is alles schouten und schreamen.

Starboard: Getderhell ausser der Strausse.

Spinnaker: Die Windebagge unterhulldragen.

Outboard Engine: Der spitzenpopper Seebootpuscher.

A young man and his wife were returning home from an extensive tour through Europe, during which they had made many excursions. As they were going through customs, an officer routinely asked if the man had anything to declare. 'Yes,' he answered. 'Bankruptcy.'

Grace is God making sure that you get what you don't deserve.

Mercy is God making sure that you don't get what you do deserve.

A neurotic is a person who builds a castle in the air.
A psychotic is the person who lives in it.
A psychiatrist is the one who collects the rent.

A patient went to his doctor for a check-up and the doctor wrote out a prescription for him in his usual illegible handwriting.

The patient put it in his pocket, but forgot to have it filled.

Every morning for two years he showed it to the

conductor as a railway pass. Twice it got him into the movies, once into the rugby stadium and once into a symphony concert.

He got an increase at work by showing it to the cashier as a note from the boss.

One day he mislaid it. His daughter picked it up, played it on the piano and won a music scholarship at a conservatory.

Once upon a time, there was a little red hen who scratched about the barnyard until she uncovered some grains of wheat. She called her neighbours and said, 'If we plant this wheat, we shall have bread to eat. Who will help me plant it?'

'Not I,' said the cow.

'Not I,' said the duck.

'Not I,' said the pig.

'Not I,' said the goose.

'Then I will,' said the little red hen, and she did. The wheat grew tall and ripened into golden grain.

'Who will help me reap my wheat?' asked the little red hen.

'Not I,' said the duck.

'Out of my classification,' said the pig.

'I'd lose my seniority,' said the cow.

'I'd lose my unemployment compensation,' said the goose.

'Then I will,' said the little red hen, and she did.

At last, it was time to bake the bread.' Who will help me bake the bread?' asked the little red hen.

'That would be overtime for me,' said the cow.

'I'd lose my welfare benefits,' said the duck.

'I'm a dropout and never learned how,' said the pig.

'If I'm to be the only helper, that's discrimination,' said the goose.

'Then I will,' said the little red hen. She baked five loaves and held them up for her neighbours to see.

They all wanted some – in fact, demanded a share. But the little red hen said, 'No, I can eat the five loaves myself.'

'Excess profits!' yelled the cow.

'Capitalist leech!' cried the duck.

'I demand equal rights!' shouted the goose.

The pig just grunted.

Then they hurriedly painted 'unfair' picket signs and

marched around, shouting obscenities.

The government agent came and said to the little red hen, 'You must not be greedy.'

'But I earned the bread,' said the little red hen.

'Exactly,' said the agent. 'That is the wonderful free-enterprise system. Anyone in the barnyard can earn as much as he wants. But, under government regulations the productive workers must 'divide their product with the idle.'

And they lived happily ever after. But the little red hen's neighbours wondered why she never again baked bread.

Nation's Business (The Chamber of Commerce of the United States)

A housewife called out with a frown
When surprised by some callers from town,
   'In a minute or less
   I'll slip on a dress'
But she slipped on the stairs and came down.

An indolent vicar of Bray
His roses allowed to decay.
   His wife, more alert,
   Bought a powerful squirt,
And said to her spouse, 'Let us spray.'

Langford Reed

She frowned and called him Mr
Because in sport he kr
   And so, in spite
   That very night
This Mr kr sr

Fangs a Lot

'The soldiers now left in Flagstaff House, residence of the former President, are, I am told, eating their way through his private zoo,' reported a columnist in a West African magazine. Full details were hard to come by, but the report set correspondents and writers to speculation about what might be going on in the cages of Kwame Nkrumah's private zoo.

Somehow the old eland was missing. Neither hide nor hair had been seen of him since the day that Kwame Nkrumah had been ostrichized, accused of being the biggest cheetah in Ghana, but safaris anyone knew, no fowl play was involved.

The first sign that anything was cooking at Flagstaff House came when Lieut General Joseph Ankrah got on the horn and was told by the operator: 'I'm sorry, the lion is busy.' 'Rhino what you're up to,' he roared, with the phone still Ringling in his ears, 'but I don't know what vulture doing it for.' In a frightful stew, Ankrah headed for the waterfront zoo (known as Hyenaspoort) for an on-the-spots investigation.

The bear facts, as Ankrah herd them, suggested that the garrison had been reluctant at first about eating up the zoo. But hesitation quickly gave way to hunger, and it soon became a matter of gibbon take. For the first time

that they could remember, the ill-paid troops at Flagstaff House were all in plover.

To some, of course, it was spoor sportsmanship, killing defenceless animals and all, but Nkrumah had made chimps of his soldiers too long, and they had lots of bones to pick. The animals, they decided were fair game. So while Nkrumah sat in Conakry, turning himself into a Guinea pig and pondering whether he should pack his trunk and join his friend Nasser at his Nile perch, the boared soldiers decided what they needed was some good gnus. One night when they were all croc-ed, they turned the zoo into Nkrumah's Bar and Gorilla.

It was aardvark. One apprentice cook was kept beesy

making hamster sandwiches, but he won no kudus for his efforts; the troops were looking for fancier fare, such as peppered leopard or antelope with cantaloupe. The troops washed down their meals with giraffes of wine, and afternoon visitors to Flagstaff House were offered tea and simbathigh, followed by lemon meringue python.

By the time Ankrah arrived on the scene, the zoo was nearly empty. Why hadn't someone phoned to inform him, he growled. 'We orangutang but ewe did not answer,' the zookeeper replied tsetsely. After a half-hearted tour of the cages, he returned to headquarters, sank wearily into a chair and, realizing it was too late to save the animals, told the garrison commander to allow his troops to continue the feast. 'As a matter of fact,' said Ankrah, 'as long as you're up, get me Grant's gazelle.'

Extract from *Time,* Ghana, 1966

'Dear Sir, with reference to your letter re Majorca tour, the flight you mention is completely booked, but we will inform you immediately someone falls out, as usually happens.'

Letter from a travel agency

French women have vivacity and chic; Italian, a natural elegance; Spanish, innocence and dignity; Austrian, especially the Viennese, a tender, intimate charm; and the English, of course, have strong and well-developed teeth.

Sunday Chronicle

A bottle of perfume that Willie sent
Was highly displeasing to Millicent
   Her thanks were so cold
   That they quarrelled, I'm told,
Through that silly scent Willie sent Millicent.

The sermon our Pastor Rt. Rev.
Began, may have had a rt. clev.,
   But his talk, though consistent,
   Kept the end so far distant
That we left since we felt he mt. nev.

A certain young chap named Bill Beebee
Was in love with a lady named Phoebe.
   'But', said he, 'I must see
   What the clerical fee
Be before Phoebe be Phoebe B Beebee.'

Carolyn Wells

'I had rather it should be asked why I had not a statue,
than why I had one.'

Cato

'I haven't met your husband; what's he like?'

'Just the ordinary type; forty-two around the waist, forty-two around the chest; ninety-two around the golf course, and a nuisance around the house.'

Newcastle Journal

'You look, Mr Shaw, as though you were enjoying yourself at this party.'

'I'm glad I do, because it's the only thing I *am* enjoying.'

'I am delighted to meet you,' said the father of a college student to a professor. 'My boy took algebra from you last year.'

'Pardon me,' replied the professor. 'Your boy was exposed to it, but he didn't take it.'

An Australian girl holidaying in London spotted this house rule on a youth hostel notice board:

'Australians and Americans are requested to be in bed by 2am; Germans are requested not to rise before 6am; Italians are requested not to sing after 10pm; Frenchmen are asked not to argue before 10am.

The instructor at a YWCA charm course was urging her students to give their escorts every chance to be gallant. 'Remain seated in the car until he has had time to step round and open the door for you,' she said. Then bowing to reality, she added, 'But if he's already in the restaurant and starting to order, don't wait any longer!'

⌐

Two camera addicts were draped over a bar in Paris, one telling the other of an experience he had had that morning.

In the Bois de Boulogne he had noticed an old crone huddled beneath a bundle of rags. Hungry and homeless, she told him the heart-breaking story of her life. Once a countess, and beautiful, she had been the toast of the continent. But step by step she lost everything and was now a wretched old woman with nothing to live for.

'The poor thing,' said the other photographer. 'What did you give her?'

'Well, it was sunny,' said the first photographer, 'so I gave her f/11 at 1/100.'

The newly rich businessman went to the sales and bought himself a racehorse. Soon afterwards the horse fell sick and he called in the vet.

'Do you think I'll be able to race him soon?' he asked the vet.

'Sure,' he replied, 'and you'll probably beat him too.'

Complaints of the Common Husband

Pool-iomyelitis
Attacks its victim first post on Monday morning, giving rise to a high fever by mid-week and reaching the 'crisis' stage by Saturday evening, when entire household is compelled to silence during the reading of the sports results. In 999 cases out of 1,000, deep depression follows.

Dishpepsia
A complaint which gives the patient such overwhelming satisfaction from giving his wife a hand with the dishes that he considers himself automatically absolved from any other jobs.

Gastro-energitis

Patient appears to be in a coma until a meal is announced, whereupon he immediately leaps to his feet to finish a half-done job.

Posterior Fire-brositis

A winter complaint in which the victim appears to feel the cold in only one part of his anatomy.

Lowbar Pneumonia

Internal dampness due to exposure to too many draughts in low pubs.

Housemaid's Knee
The one not reserved for his secretary.

Not-sleeping Sickness
A morbid desire to sleep in trains and armchairs accompanied by a delusion that the patient 'only shut his eyes for a moment'.

Collar-blindness
The patient seems unable to see things which have been put in the proper place, in particular, collars, socks and handkerchiefs.

Skirtsophrenia
Obsession with hem-lines, waistlines and plunging necklines.

Manner-allergy
The patient divests himself of his good manners along with his overcoat when entering his own home.

Ashtigmatism
Inability to see an ashtray, however large or prominently placed.

Status Emphaticus
A condition in which the patient believes everyone else to be wrong.

Sleep Paralysis
Severe attacks occur when it is the patient's turn to attend to the baby crying in the night.

Sceptiseemis
A feigned condition which closes the mind to any hint that prices are high, and that last year's dress isn't what he should be content to see his wife wear.

Kettle Rash
Tendency to want cups of tea continuously.

Resex Action
The involuntary response of the average husband on meeting any other female.

Garden-cephalitis Lethargica
Seasonal malady making the male allergic to weeds and lawn-mowers.

Gilt Complex
Preoccupation with saving money *on the housekeeping.*

Delusions of Mandeur
An automatic assumption that, because men are masculine, they are more accurate, broad-minded, capable, dependable, energetic, forbearing, generous, logical, orderly, punctual, resourceful, shrewd, thorough, unselfish, wise and wonderful than women.

In the country town of Chatsworth, in Queensland, Australia, an inspector visited the bank and found it open, but deserted. Looking out of the back window, he spotted the manager, cashier, accountant and ledger-keeper playing poker – with their own money – on the landing. Hoping to scare the erring quartet, he set off the burglar alarm. But at this signal the bartender from a nearby pub rushed across the street carrying four beers.

In a crowded bus one day, a fellow was surprised when the attractive young lady across the aisle smiled at him. And his face turned a bright shade of red when, in a pleasant but loud voice, she asked, 'Aren't you the father of two of my children?'

'Why, well – that is. I'm not sure. I mean, I don't know.'

'I'm sure you are,' she said. 'I teach fourth grade at Washington School.'

THE COURSE OF TRUE LOVE

Early Stages

'Darling you look so frail and feminine in that dress.'

'I worried all night about our quarrel, please forgive me.'

'Any night next week I can make myself free.'

'Let's go somewhere quiet where we won't see anyone we know.'

'I'll pick you up at your office and drive you home.'

'You must come to Florence while I'm there.'

'Let's go home before we have to give someone a lift.'

'I missed you three times at the office. I was in a panic.'

Closing Stages

'Help me move that sofa over there, will you?'

'You seem to delight in making scenes.'

'You will have to make it Tuesday or Friday.'

'This place has gone off, not a soul I know.'

'Come round to my flat at 8.30pm and don't be late.'

'See you when I get back from Italy.'

'Anybody want a lift?'

'I did ring you up the day before yesterday, but you weren't there.'

'Taxi, darling?'

'Hardly worth taking a cab; it's only a step.'

'Please wear that dress again, I could look at you in it for ever.'

'Do me a favour, will you? When you get home throw that dress out. I never want to see it again.'

'Here's a present for you darling, they're nylons.'

'Any use for these?'

'Champagne?'

'Lager?'

Anne Edwards in the *Daily Express,* 1952

As two teachers walked along the school corridor, two small boys approached them, one talking explosively to the other. The teachers were about to pass them when one shouted, 'Sometimes me gran'muvver makes me so bloomin' wild I feel like cuttin' 'er froat!'

One teacher stopped and eyed the boy as only a schoolteacher can.

'The word,' she said, 'is throat, not froat!'

⌐

Sir William (Billy) Butlin, Britain's holiday camp king, told this story of the day he called in at his Skegness holiday camp one summer. The camp was full, and an old man and an elderly lady were being turned away by the harassed receptionist. Anxious to help, Butlin explained that he would not be using his own chalet that week and told the receptionist to assign it to the couple.

Returning the following week, Butlin found the elderly lady at his chalet, full of gratitude. Yes, it had been a lovely holiday – the food, the accommodation, the entertainment were all wonderful. 'There's only one thing,' she added confidentially. 'I don't much like that old man you put in here with me.'

There was a man who, to the consternation of his wife and daughter, would never go to a doctor. His method was self-diagnosis – which meant he often purloined medicines intended for other members of the family. When he was in his 80s, his daughter was suspicious that he was taking her tonic and she asked him about it. He admitted he was, so she thought she would try to stop him by saying, 'But it's for female trouble.'

'Good'; he replied testily, 'I've got plenty of that too.'

⌒

Recently, at a ship's cocktail party, a rating noticed that a row of coat-hooks outside the wardroom was marked: 'Officers Only'.

Underneath someone had scrawled: 'Can also be used for coats'.

Moving into a new house can be tricky, especially if you are accident-prone. Take the case of a man who moved into a new house in the suburbs.

One night, soon after he and his wife moved in, he was awakened by loudly clanging bells: the burglar alarm had gone off.

Grabbing his revolver he leapt out of bed and – the house still being strange to him – ran briskly through a glass panel separating the lounge from the dining room.

He suffered numerous cuts – fortunately none of them serious – which required attention. His wife telephoned for an ambulance, which took him to hospital. To occupy herself while her husband was gone she set about clearing up the mess, and, finding that water would not remove the bloodstains from her new floor, she poured some benzine into a container and cleaned up with that.

Having done this she disposed of the benzine by pouring it down the toilet, omitting, however, to flush it.

Some hours later, her stitched and bandaged husband returned. Not feeling like bed for the moment, he decided to visit the toilet. Once comfortably seated he lit a cigarette, no doubt hoping that it would soothe his nerves. The effect, alas, was the opposite. He dropped the still-burning match into he pan.

Instantly there was a violent explosion followed by a sheet of flame.

Dragging her dazed, shocked, and quite extensively burnt husband out of the scene of the explosion, the lady again ran to the telephone and dialled a number which she had not yet had time to forget.

Some confusion resulted, the ambulance department maintaining that her husband had already been returned, but eventually they realized that this was a second 'happening', and again they sent the ambulance.

Strong hands gently placed the smouldering husband on the stretcher and the ambulancemen carried him outside for the second time, lost their way in the dark and wandered into the rockery.

Among the stones, somebody's foot slipped and the injured man was tipped off on to the rockery, breaking his collarbone.

There once was a choleric colonel,
Whose oaths were obscene and infolonel,
    And the Chaplain, aghast,
    Gave up protest at last,
But wrote them all down in his jolonel.

Said a bad little youngster named Beauchamp,
'Those jelly tarts, how shall I reauchamp?
    To my parents I'd go,
    But they always say "No",
No matter how much I beseauchamp.'

A tutor who tooted the flute,
Tried to tutor two tooters to toot.
    Said the two to the tutor,
    'Is it harder to toot, or
To tutor two tooters to toot?'

One of the German guards at a prisoner of war camp, in World War Two, was a keen cyclist. The day the Battle of Britain started, the guard hurried into one of the huts.

'The war will soon be over,' he announced. 'Then I will make a tour of the new German empire on my bicycle.'

'And what,' queried a bored voice from one of the bunks, 'will you do in the afternoon?'

⌒

Weekend golfer Martin Robertson – handicap 18 – drove into golfing history with a drive that almost shot down a low flying Royal Navy jet.

From the ninth hole at Moray, Lossiemouth, he scored a direct hit on a Hunter fighter, as it came in to land at the Royal Naval air station nearby.

The ball hit a wing, but the plane landed safely. The Navy said later that the consequences could have been 'disastrous', and added:

'All our aircraft returned safely to base. It is understood that one of their golf balls is missing.'

WAITER, THERE'S A FLY
IN MY SOUP

1 It's all right, sir, it won't live long in that stuff.
2 Don't worry, he'll sink when he's dead.
3 He's slow, the rest are on the second course.
4 It must have committed insecticide.
5 Yes, sir, it's the bad meat that attracts them.
6 Would you prefer it served separately?
7 Yes, sir, it's the flavour of the month.
8 That's funny, most people find cockroaches.
9 Yes, sir, we're out of garlic.

10 The dog must have missed it.

11 Sorry, sir, I've had him out once.

12 What do you expect for £1.50, roast beef?

13 Don't be alarmed, those sort aren't dangerous.

14 Leave it there, the goldfish will eat it.

15 So that's where they go in winter.

16 Isn't it cooked the way you like it?

17 I'll fetch you a spider.

18 What's the matter? You a vegetarian?

19 No extra charge.

20 Isn't it sad when they die so young.

21 If you throw him a pea he'll play water polo.

22 Don't put him on the cloth, his feet are all wet

23 Yes, they practise high diving from the ceiling.

24 I'm not superstitious.

25 So what!

26 Don't worry, sir, he won't drink it all.

27 Don't eat it, sir, it's only for decoration.

28 Fascinating creatures, aren't they?

29 Not to worry, sir, he'll dissolve in a few minutes.

30 I'll get him a spoon.

31 It's all right, it's not deep enough to drown him.

32 Don't worry, sir, all our soups are treated with DDT.

33 They have to keep warm somehow.

34 Don't wave your spoon about, sir, you'll frighten him.

THE CHURCHILL TOUCH

At a reception during the war, an American woman was questioning Winston Churchill.

'What are you going to do about those wretched Indians?' she asked.

'Madam,' he replied courteously, 'To which Indians do you refer? Do you refer to the second greatest nation on earth, which under benign and munificent British rule has multiplied and prospered exceedingly? Or to the unfortunate North American Indians which under your present administration are almost extinct?'

⤺

I was the private secretary on duty with Winston Churchill at Chequers during the last weekend of the Second World War. None of us had had much sleep for days and I was exhausted when I finally managed to stagger into bed at three in the morning. No sooner had I fallen asleep than the telephone rang. An apologetic operator said she had a top priority call from General Eisenhower's Military Assistant. His first question shook me: 'The General told me to ask you if the war is over.'

'Would you mind repeating that?' I stammered in surprise.

'No. Has the war ended? We've just received a news agency message stating categorically that the war is over. Nobody's told the General and if it *is* all over, he ought to be one of the first to know. Does the PM have any information on the subject?'

'No,' I replied stiffly. 'As far as Mr Churchill is concerned, we're still fighting.'

'So you think I'd better tell the General to carry on with the war?'

'Yes, I think it would be advisable.'

'OK. Good night and sorry to bother you.'

'Not a bit. Good night.'

John Peck, Churchill's Secretary

Filling out endless forms is accepted as inevitable but every so often the worm turns. A builder constructing a small factory at Andover in Hampshire, sent a blueprint to the County Planning Committee.

Complying with committee orders that all factories must have flower beds, the architect indicated a space for 'shrubs'. The plan came back to the builder with a question: what kind of plants did the builder intend planting?

Back to the committee went the reply: he was planning to grow *Urtica dioica, Calystegia sepium, Rumex obtusifolius* and *Taraxacum officinale*. The county council stamped his application 'approved'. Apparently none of the commitee realized that what the builder proposed to plant were stinging nettles, bindweed, dock and dandelion.

Six well-known citizens were named as pall-bearers in the will of a man who died penniless and owing them considerable sums. 'They have been wonderful creditors,' the will said, 'and I would like them to carry me to the end.'

⤶

A number of old sayings make more sense if you just drop the last word. For instance: familiarity breeds; dead men don't; money is the root of all; fools rush in where angels fear to; beauty is only skin; hell hath no fury like a woman.

⤶

A lecturer in English at an American university introduced his class to what he considered to be 'one of the finest, most elegant lines of poetry in the English language.' He had duly recorded it in all of his notebooks as a constant reminder of its beauty. 'Walk with light!' he quoted, and then repeated softly and blissfully to himself 'Walk with light . . . now isn't that a wonderful thing to say to someone?' The class agreed, of course, and wished to know the author.

'I suppose it's anonymous,' said the instructor. 'It's written on a sign at a street intersection in the town.'

There was a young fellow named Tait,
Who dined with his girl at 8.08.
   But I'd hate to relate
   What that fellow named Tait
And his *tête-a-tête* ate at 8.08.

All things bright and beautiful,
All creatures great and small,
All things wise and wonderful,
Commercials kill them all.

Each little flower that opens,
Each little bird that sings,
Relates to body odours
Or crow's feet, lines and rings.

CHORUS

The purple-headed mountain,
The river running by,
Bring news of constipation
Or pre-cooked kidney pie.

CHORUS

The cold wind in the winter,
The pleasant summer sun,
Mean gobs of turgid ketchup,
Or margariny bun.

CHORUS

The tall trees in the greenwood,
The meadows where we play,
Promote elastic stockings
And keep bad breath away.

CHORUS

They give us eyes to see them,
And lips that we might tell
How God was in his heaven,
Till commerce made it hell.

CHORUS

Frank Caber

A canner, exceedingly canny,
One morning remarked to his granny:
   'A canner can can
   Anything that he can,
But a canner can't can a can, can he?'

Carolyn Wells

A rocket explorer named Wright
Once travelled much faster than light.
   He set out one day
   In a relative way,
And returned on the previous night.

There was a young maiden of Siam
Who said to her lover, young Kiam,
   'If you kiss me, of course
   You will have to use force,
But thank goodness you're stronger than I am.'

When the civil engineer took advantage
of a lovely young lady from Wantage,
    The county surveyor
    Said, 'You'll have to pay her,
For you've altered the line of her frontage.'

William Allen White, the editor of the *Emporia Gazette*, Kansas, described his war against his staff's over-use of the word 'very' this way:

If you feel you must write 'very', write 'damn'. So, when the urge for emphasis is on him, the reporter writes, 'It was a damn fine victory. I am damn tired but damn well – and damn excited.' Then because it is the *Emporia Gazette*, the sub-editor deletes the profanity and the quotation reads. 'It was a fine victory. I am tired but well – and excited.' That's how the *Gazette* attains its restrained, simple and forceful style.

Writer's Guide and Index to English

Man is by far the cruellest of all the animals. Our vicious-ness shows in our everyday gestures. We beat eggs. We whip cream. We strike bargains. We stifle a scandal. We blind others to the truth. We violate rules. We bury our secret lives. And all the while, we are trying to kill time.

〜

Sir Alexander Fleming made his discovery of penicillin while working in a dusty old laboratory. A mould spore, which had blown in through a window, landed on a culture plate he was about to examine.

Some years later, he was taken on a tour of an up-to-date research lab., a gleaming, air-conditioned, dust-free, super-sterile setting. 'What a pity you did not have a place like this to work in,' his guide said. 'What you could have discovered in such surroundings!'

'Not penicillin,' Fleming observed dryly.

〜

While staying in Tokyo my tape recorder went wrong, so I telephoned an electronics shop to ask if they could send somebody to the hotel to put it right. 'Immediately,' they said.

After about four hours, a young man arrived in such a starchy version of European formal dress that he might have been going to a royal garden party. He must have spent three and a half of those hours hiring and dressing up in it.

He mended the recorder and then broached a subject which was obviously very much on his mind. 'What,' he asked, 'is the correct form for English people meeting for the first time?'

'Well,' I said, shifting about a bit and blushing because I always think it is the most ridiculous of all English social forms, 'they usually shake hands and one says, "How do you do," and then the other says, "How do you do," or they both say it together.'

He took this in without a smile and said, 'In what position are the feet?'

Rene Cutworth, the *Listener*, 1974

The more you give, the more you get,
The more you laugh, the less you fret,
The more you do unselfishly, the more you live
    abundantly,
The more of everything you share,
The more you'll always have to spare
The more you have, the more you'll find,
That life is good and friends are kind,
For only what we give away,
Enriches us from day to day.

Lord Birkenhead, when he was a barrister, disliked being told by judges that they had a poor opinion of his case. When one judge commented, 'I have read your case, and I am no wiser now than I was when I started,' his reply was crushing: 'Possibly not, my lord, but far better informed.'

The Wit of the Wig

The reward of energy, enterprise and thrift is taxes.

⤳

Geist's Rule for Travel with Children
    Never in the same direction.

⤳

Any country with 'democratic' in the title isn't.

⤳

THE WORLD'S WORST QUESTIONS

Will you promise not to get angry if I ask you something?
Do you have statistics to back up that statement?
You don't honestly expect me to believe that, do you?
Haven't you any sense of humour?
You don't remember me, do you?
Have I kept you waiting?
Now what's the matter?
You asleep?
So what?
When are you going to grow up?

The smallest hole will eventually empty the largest container, unless it is made intentionally for drainage, in which case it will clog.

Dave Grissom

If it wasn't for the last minute, nothing would ever get done.

The faster planes become, the longer it takes to get to the airport.

J Marais

It took only fifty years for movies to go from silent to unspeakable.

Doug Larson

Is there a difference between a fat chance and a slim chance?

⌇

Opportunity's favourite disguise is trouble.

⌇

A closed mouth catches no feet.

⌇

A flea once lived on a pheasant
   Who was royally vain and unpleasant,
'Til the flea, on a whim
   Bit the 'h' out of him
And now he's only a peasant.

Lois Lambie

I could have been
    a psychiatrist but the thought made me shrink
    a neurosurgeon but I didn't have the nerve
    a juggler but things got out of hand
    a moneylender but I lost interest
    a marksman but I didn't stick to my guns

Lani Serquina

No good deed goes unpunished.

Leakproof seals – will.

Self-starters – won't.

Interchangeable parts – won't.

Anything that can go wrong – will.

All warranties expire upon payment of invoice.

⤺

A short cut is the longest distance between two points.

⤺

The chance of a piece of bread falling with the buttered side down is directly proportional to the cost of the carpet.

⤺

No matter how long or hard you shop for an item, after you've bought it, it will be on sale somewhere cheaper.

⤺

The other lane always moves faster.

⤺

In order to get a bank loan you must first prove that you don't need it.

Anything you try to fix will take longer and cost more than you planned for.

〜

A £40 picture tube will protect a 30 pence fuse by blowing first.

〜

If it joins, force it. If it breaks it needed replacing anyway.

〜

In my dotage I have become
Inert, defunct, inane.
Oh, to be like yesteryear
Ert, funct and ane again.

Larry Burns

RULES FOR COMPANY VEHICLES – NEW SOUTH AFRICA

Due to the perks, tax on company cars and the price increase on petrol, all company cars will be replaced by bicycles.

The allocation of bicycles is as follows:

Representatives: three speed with bell.
Sales Manager: three speed with bell and pump.
Branch Manager: ten speed, two mirrors, plastic raincoat, mud flaps and choice of metallic colours.
Managing Director: tandem with chauffeur.

A notice in a club asked, 'Will any member volunteer to teach Pitman shorthand one evening a week?' To this someone added: 'I thought he knew it.'

Peterborough, *Daily Telegraph*, 1972

⌒

Have you noticed that when your arms are filled with parcels, the sign on the door always says 'Pull'?

Have you ever noticed that when a politician clarifies an earlier statement, it usually means the public understood it too well?

⌒

To accommodate the crowd of more than 5,000 people who turned up to hear Sir Edmund Hillary lecture in Victoria, Canada, a floor was built over the ice of the city arena, which created a genuinely glacial atmosphere for the chilling feats Sir Edmund would be describing.

Surveying arrangements for his projector, he turned to me and asked, 'Will it be icey or dicey?'

'Oh, I wouldn't worry about it', I replied. 'The floor covering works pretty well. People will probably have to wear coats but I don't think they'll be uncomfortable.'

This reply seemed to bewilder Hillary. 'No, no', he said. And then pointing to his projector, he repeated, 'Will it be icey or dicey?'

Finally the light dawned. What he wanted to determine was whether the arena was AC or DC.

Stuart Keate, *Paper Bay*

RULES POSTED SEPTEMBER, 1882, AT THE MACLEOD HOTEL IN ALBERTA, CANADA

(a) A deposit must be made before towels, soap or candles can be carried to rooms. When boarders are leaving, a rebate will be made on all candles or parts of candles not burned or eaten.

(b) Not more than one dog allowed to be kept in each single room.

(c) Quarrelsome or boisterous persons, also those who shoot off without provocation guns or other explosive weapons on the premises, and all boarders who get killed, will not be allowed to remain in the House.

(d) When guests find themselves or their baggage thrown over the fence, they may consider that they have received notice to leave.

(e) The proprietor will not be accountable for anything.

(f) Only regularly registered guests will be allowed the special privilege of sleeping on the Bar Room floor.

(g) Meals served in own rooms will not be guaranteed in any way. Our waiters are hungry and not above temptation.

(h) All guests are requested to rise at 6a.m. This is imperative as the sheets are needed for tablecloths.

(i) To attract the attention of waiters, shoot a hole through the door panel. Two for ice water, three shots for a deck of cards, and so on.

There are has-beans, 'yooman beans' and jelly-beans. Now there is a young man in Harare who wishes to be a tender bean.

The aspiring young would-be worker answered an advertisement in the *Herald* by an agricultural concern calling for tenders to buy the bean crop on one of their farms.

His letter said he wished to apply for the vacancy of a tender bean since he was well qualified, having his RJC in English, religious knowledge, mathematics, history and geography.

He ended by stating that he felt the post would exercise his intellectual ability and accuracy in statistics.

A salesgirl was standing on the pavement outside the local department store, demonstrating the efficiency of a window-cleaning device by smearing margarine on glass and cleaning it off again. Impressed, a middle-aged woman asked her 'How much margarine should I use?'

Margaret Stead, *Reader's Digest*, 1981

～

Do you realize that the merest titter of a sneeze will get you 'God bless you's' and *'gesundheits!'* by the score; but when you almost cough yourself to death, all you get are dirty looks?

Edward Stevenson, *Reader's Digest*, 1982